D0758609

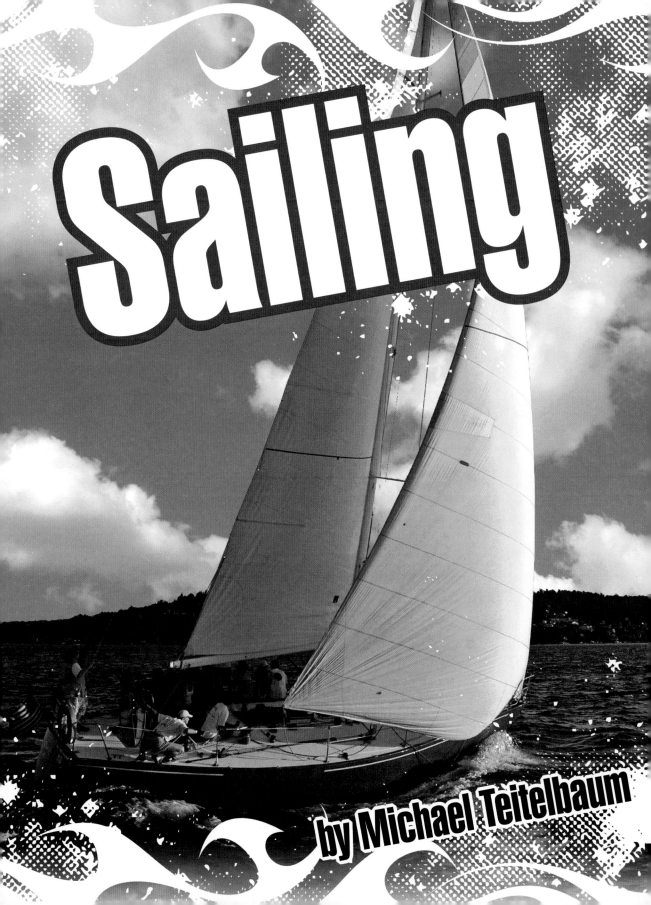

Sailing

by Michael Teitelbaum

Published by The Child's World®
1980 Lookout Drive
Mankato, MN 56003-1705
800-599-READ
www.childsworld.com

The Child's World®: Mary Berendes, Publishing Director
Shoreline Publishing Group, LLC: James Buckley Jr.,
    Production Director
The Design Lab: Design and production

ISBN 9781609731847
LCCN 2011928874

Photo credits: Cover: dreamstime.com/Tom Dowd.
Interior: AP/Wide World: 7, 24, 27; dreamstime.com:
Alexander Lvov 4, Ron Zmiri 8, Mikael Damkier 12,
Gemphotography 15, Heysue23 16, Modhaka 19,
Alberto Dubini 23, Shawn Jackson 28; iStock: 11, 20.

Printed in the United States of America

Table of Contents

Huge sailing ships roamed the world's oceans for centuries.

CHAPTER ONE

Powered by Wind

You race across the water. Your boat slices through the foamy white sea as you speed ahead. But you have no motor. You have no oars. You are powered only by the wind. You are sailing!

Humans have been using sails on boats to capture the force of the wind for thousands of years. The ancient Egyptians built ships with one large **mast** that held an enormous sail. These ships carried hundreds of people on voyages of exploration or war.

During the **Middle Ages**, Arab, Chinese, Indian, and European explorers sailed the seas to learn about faraway places. They sailed through extreme weather and into dangerous ocean conditions. They had nothing but their wooden ships and cloth sails to carry them.

Today people sail for fun and recreation. Sailing has also become a competitive sport. It is featured in the **Olympics**.

The America's Cup is one of the most famous sailing races. This race has become one of the world's longest running sporting events. The first Cup was awarded in 1851. (The most recent winner was *BMW Oracle*, from the United States, which won in 2010.)

Sailors describe the sensation of sailing as leaving the real world. They are cut off from land and people, carried along only by the wind and their own skills at steering their boats. Some sailors say they feel as if they have entered a private world of their own as they move through the water.

BMW Oracle (right) leads in the 2010 America's Cup race over a boat from Italy.

Strong winds and rough seas can be a challenge for sailors.

Every sailing trip, short or long, on a river, an ocean, or a lake, presents its own challenges. Weather plays a big part in the safety and success of a sailing trip. How the water is acting affects a sailing voyage as well.

Is the ocean calm or **choppy**? Big waves can be a dangerous challenge for even the most experienced sailor. Good judgment and knowledge about their boat can help sailors weather most storms. These qualities are also the key to enjoying this sport. Sailors also must learn to use only the wind to steer and move their boats.

But what exactly is a sailboat? They come in all shapes and size. However, the next pages give you a short tour around a standard sailboat. The next chapter explains more about these important parts.

Speaking Sailing

Sailboats and sailors have their own language. When learning about sailing, you should know some of the key words that you'll read and hear. Here are some common sailing terms. Some have to do with directions, others with parts of the boats.

1. **Aft**—back of a sailboat, also called the "stern"

2. **Boom**—horizontal pole which extends from the bottom of the mast; it helps the sailor move the sail so it best catches the wind

3. **Bow**—(rhymes with *wow*) front of a sailboat

4. **Leeward**—(pronounced LOO-urd) the opposite direction to the direction in which the wind is blowing

5. **Mast**—large wooden pole that extends up from the center of a sailboat

6. **Port**—left side of a sailboat (when facing the bow)

7. **Rudder**—a flat piece of wood, fiberglass, or metal beneath or at the back of the boat that is used for steering

8. **Starboard**—right side of a sailboat (when facing the bow)

9. **Windward**—the direction the wind is blowing

Use the numbers to find the parts of the sailing ship.

CHAPTER TWO

What's on a Sailboat?

Although there are many different kinds of sailboats, the basic parts of all sailboats are the same. They include the mast, the main sail, the jib or head sail, the boom, and the rudder.

The mast is the large wooden pole that extends up from the center of the boat. The boom is another wooden pole that runs horizontally from the bottom of the mast. The boom holds the bottom of the sail. The main sail provides the most wind power. The jib helps capture wind that gets around the main sail. The rudder helps steer the sailboat.

Look for the mast, the main sail, and the jib on this boat.

The different types of sailboats include sloops, cutters, yawls, ketches, and schooners. The main differences among the various types of sailboats are the number of masts and where the masts are on the boat.

A sloop has one large, tall mast in the middle. Two sails are attached to that mast, the main sail and the jib. The main sail is larger than the jib.

A cutter has its mast farther toward the aft section of the boat. Yawls and ketches are sailboats that have two masts. These tend to be bigger boats.

One of the most popular and inexpensive types of sailboats is the Sunfish. The Sunfish is a small craft with one mast. The boat can only carry one or two people. The Sunfish first appeared in 1952. It's easy to launch from a beach, sending the sailor off on an ocean adventure without going too far from shore.

The Sunfish is easy to
launch from the beach.

The captain stays at the wheel to steer his sailboat.

Sailboats are steered using the rudder. This flat piece of wood, fiberglass, or metal acts the way an oar works in a rowboat. The flat part of the rudder stays in the water under the boat. The handle of the rudder is above the water and is controlled by the person steering the sailboat.

Here's the tricky part. The person working the rudder must move the handle in the *opposite* direction from the direction in which he or she wants the boat to turn. It takes a little getting used to, but soon enough, steering the rudder, like all parts of sailing becomes second nature.

Most larger boats have steering wheels, or helms, that work like a car, making steering easier.

When the wind is blowing in the direction you want to sail, smooth sailing is just a matter of catching the wind in your sails. The wind will push you in a straight line.

But what about when the wind is not cooperating?

Sailors **tack** to help the wind push them in the right direction—even if the wind is not blowing that way. Tacking means that the sailboat goes back and forth in a zigzag pattern in order to go from one point to another. The wind pushes the boat to the side, but also in the right direction, although not in a straight line.

Boat crews move the sails to catch the wind.

Everyone in small sailboats should wear a life jacket.

Emergencies can always pop up on a sailboat. As the captain of the boat, you may not have time to tell your guests what to do if an emergency is taking place. Because of this, it's important to let them know what to do before trouble occurs.

Make sure all guests have a PFD (personal **flotation** device). Also, everyone on a sailboat should know how to quickly slow the boat. This can be done by releasing the sails so that they no longer catch the wind.

Everyone on board should know where the boat's fire extinguishers are located. They should also know how to operate the radio to call for help if needed.

Regardless of the type of sailboat you sail, safety is the number one factor. All sailors have a safety checklist they go through before leaving dry land.

Safety Checklist
- Check the weather forecast
- Check local wind and wave conditions
- Always let someone know where you will be sailing, what time you expect to go there, and what time you expect to return.
- Make sure all guests on your sailboat have the right sailing gear, including rubber-soled shoes to grip the deck.
- Show your guests what to do in emergencies.

CHAPTER THREE

Hoist that Sail!

Long ago, people sailed for **commerce** and trade, to explore new lands, or to wage war. Today, most people sail for recreation and fun. Sailing is also a competitive sport—and an exciting one at that!

The Inter-Collegiate Sailing Association runs sailing as a college sport. Since 1937, they have held championship races in six different categories. The Singlehanded competition (one race for men and one for women) involves one person operating a small sailboat. The other races include a sloop competition, several competitions on dinghies (very small boats with a single sail), and several team races.

The United States Sailing Association is in charge of major sailing races throughout the country. They deal with yacht racing, dinghy racing, and windsurfing.

A crowd of sailboats heads out for a race.

Sarah Ayton steered this boat to a 2004 Olympic gold medal.

Another Way to Sail

Windsurfing combines sailing and surfing. Instead of flying above a boat, the sail is attached to a kind of surfboard. The rider stands on the board and turns the sail to catch the wind. Windsurfers glide along on the ocean's surface, riding the surfboard. They can also jump up and over waves or even do flips.

Sailing has been an Olympic sport since 1908. The events included one-person sailing, two-person sailing, and most recently windsurfing has become an Olympic sailing event.

One Olympic couple from England has a bunch of sailing medals between them. Nick Dempsey won the bronze medal in windsurfing in 2008. His wife, Sarah Ayton, is a two-time Olympic sailing champion. She captured the gold in 2004 and 2008. In 2012, Nick, however, will try to better his bronze medal. He'll go for gold when the Olympics are held in his home country.

Krystal Weir of Australia is one of the best sailors in the world. She won a world championship in 2004, was a teammate of Sarah Ayton in 2008, and is hoping for a run at gold in 2012. Weir has long been regarded at the best female sailor in her home country.

Most sailors enjoy taking their boats out for a day trip. But the most extreme sailors have actually sailed around the world!

The first person to sail around the world alone was Joshua Slocum. Born in Nova Scotia in 1844, Slocum moved to America and became a sea captian at the age of 25. In 1895, at the age of 51, Slocum sailed out of Boston on his 37-foot (11-m) sloop named *Spray*.

Slocum crossed the Atlantic, but steered away from the Mediterranean when when he was warned of pirates there. Slocum sailed around South America, Australia, and back across the Atlantic.

In 1898, three years and 46,000 miles (74,000 km) later, he landed at Newport, Rhode Island, the first person to sail solo around the world.

More recently, in 2010, 16-year-old Jessica Watson became the youngest person to sail solo around the world. Watson spent seven months at sea sailing her pink yacht.

Jessica Watson took 210 days to sail her pink boat around the world . . . alone!

Slocum and Watson were extreme sailors. Most people sail close to home on lakes, rivers, or near the seashore. Young sailors learn in classes, working their way up from very small boats to larger and larger ones.

Sailing courses teach sailing skills and safety. Skills include how to use the boat's sails to keep you moving in the direction in which you want to go. Students learn how to tie knots in a sailboat's ropes, along with how to dock and anchor (or park) the sailboat. In safety lessons, they learn about sailing gear, how to read weather, and how to use a boat's radio.

Whatever kind of sailboat you choose, the object is always the same—to catch the wind and go for a ride.

Sailing can lead to amazing views like this one.

Glossary

choppy—condition of the sea when the ocean makes many small, but powerful waves

commerce—business

flotation—ability to ride on top of water

mast—the large wooden pole that extends up from the center of a sailboat

Middle Ages—the period in European history from the 5th century to the 15th century

Olympics—an international athletic competition, that takes place every four years, in which many of the world's nations compete.

tack—the process of turning a sailboat so that the sails best catch the wind

Find Out More

BOOKS

The Little Sailboat
By Lois Lenski (Random House, 2003)
A sweet story about a sailboat voyage.

Sailing for Kids
By Gary Kibble (Wiley, 2006)
Basic information about sailing.

Sarah's Boat
By Douglass Alvord (Tilbury House, 2001)
A story that also gives basic sailing information.

WEB SITES

For links to learn more about extreme sports: **childsworld.com/links**

Note to Parents, Teachers, and Librarians: We routinely verify our Web links to make sure they are safe and active sites. So encourage your readers to check them out!

Index

About the Author

Michael Teitelbaum has been a writer and editor of children's books and magazines for more than twenty years. He was editor of several kids' magazines and also wrote *Jackie Robinson: Champion For Equality*. Michael's fiction includes *The Scary States of America* and *Backyard Sports*.